A+
books

Animal Opposites

short
and
TALL

An Animal Opposites Book

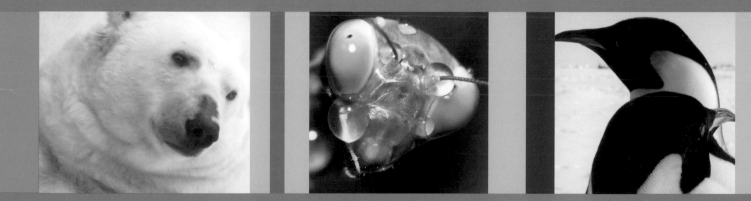

by Nathan Olson

Capstone
press
Mankato, Minnesota

Some animals are short enough to hide in grass and brush. Other animals are tall enough to reach the tops of trees.

2

Let's learn about short and tall by looking at animals around the world.

short

Badgers need to be short to chase their prey through holes and burrows. They are fierce fighters.

TALL

Giraffes need to be tall to eat leaves from the highest branches They are peaceful plant-eaters.

Giraffes sleep standing up. They sleep on their feet in case they need to run away from danger.

short

Ermines are short arctic animals. They can chase rabbits and mice through underground tunnels.

An ermine's coat is brown in the spring and summer. It turns white in the winter.

TALL

Polar bears are tall arctic animals. They stand up on their hind legs and smell the air to find prey.

Polar bears have black skin under their white fur. The dark color draws in heat from the sun and helps keep them warm.

short

Shetland ponies are short.
But they are strong enough
to give you a ride.

Horses stand tall. Some baby horses, called foals, are as tall as a full-grown pony.

TALL

9

short

Penguins are birds with very short legs. There is just enough room for a chick to keep warm.

TALL

Ostriches cannot fly. They use their wings for balance when they run.

The ostrich is the tallest bird in the world. It stands almost 8 feet (2.4 meters) tall.

short

Dachshunds are very short dogs. They can be shorter than a cat.

TALL

Great Danes
stand quite tall.
They are as tall
as a pony.

short

With no legs at all, snakes are
short enough to easily hide.

TALL

Cobras can be tall snakes. They rise up if they sense danger.

short

Even though centipedes have lots of legs, they are still short bugs.

Praying mantises have only six legs. But they are tall bugs.

Praying mantises can eat small tree frogs.

short

Egrets have short feathers
fanning out on their heads.

18

Peacocks proudly fan their tall, colorful tail feathers.

short

Horned lizards use their short horns to dig in the sand and hide.

TALL

Elk have tall, strong antlers that they use for fighting.

short

Hawkfish are short.
They hide in coral.

22

TALL

Sea rods grow tall. These corals look like plants. But they are really animals.

short

Baby gorillas are short.
Some are even shorter than
human babies at birth.

TALL

Gorillas walk with their knuckles on the ground.

Gorillas grow into tall adults. Standing up, male gorillas are taller than some human adults.

Short animals can chase prey into small places. Others can easily hide when in danger. Some tall animals run away from enemies. Others use their height to stay safe.

What kinds of short and tall
animals live near you?

Did You Know?

A full-grown male giraffe can stand as tall as 18 feet (5.5 meters), which makes it the world's tallest animal. An adult giraffe's neck can weigh as much as 600 pounds (272 kilograms).

A group of gorillas is called a troop. Who is tallest in the troop? The male silverback gorilla is taller and almost twice as heavy as the females.

Peacocks use their tall feathers to attract females, called peahens. Peahens do not have colorful feathers.

Penguins spend most of their lives in the water. They use their short wings, legs, and feet to swim.

Why do snakes flick out their tongues? There is a special organ in a snake's mouth that helps it to smell. The tongue brings different smells into the mouth.

Glossary

balance (BAL-uhnss) — the ability to keep steady and not fall over

burrow (BUR-oh) — a tunnel or hole in the ground made or used by a rabbit, badger, or other animal

coral (KOR-uhl) — an ocean animal with a soft body and many tentacles; corals often live in groups.

danger (DAYN-jur) — a situation that is not safe

enemy (EN-uh-mee) — a person or animal that wants to harm or destroy another

foal (FOHL) — a young horse

knuckle (NUHK-uhl) — one of the joints in a finger

prey (PRAY) — an animal that is hunted by another animal for food

Read More

Bullard, Lisa. *Long and Short: An Animal Opposites Book.* A+ Books: Animal Opposites. Mankato, Minn.: Capstone Press, 2006.

Got, Yves. *Sam's Opposites.* San Francisco: Chronicle Books, 2003.

Hall, Kirsten. *Oops!: All About Opposites.* New York: Children's Press, 2003.

Internet Sites

FactHound offers a safe, fun way to find Internet sites related to this book. All of the sites on FactHound have been researched by our staff.

Here's how:

1. Visit *www.facthound.com*

2. Choose your grade level.

3. Type in this book ID **1429612126** for age-appropriate sites. You may also browse subjects by clicking on letters, or by clicking on pictures and words.

4. Click on the **Fetch It** button.

FactHound will fetch the best sites for you!

Index

A+ Books are published by Capstone Press,
151 Good Counsel Drive, P.O. Box 669, Mankato, Minnesota 56002.
www.capstonepress.com

1 2 3 4 5 6 13 12 11 10 09 08

Library of Congress Cataloging-in-Publication Data
Olson, Nathan.
    Short and tall: an animal opposites book / by Nathan Olson.
    p. cm. — (A+ books. Animal opposites)
    Includes bibliographical references and index.
    ISBN-13: 978-1-4296-1212-8 (hardcover)
    ISBN-10: 1-4296-1212-6 (hardcover)
    1. Animals — Juvenile literature. 2. Body size — Juvenile literature. I. Title. II. Series.
QL799.3.O47 2008
591.4'1 — dc22   2007036219

Summary: Brief text introduces the concepts of short and tall, comparing some of the
    world's shortest and tallest animals.

Credits
Heather Adamson and Megan Peterson, editors; Veronica Bianchini and
    Renée T. Doyle, designers; Wanda Winch, photo researcher

Photo Credits
BigStockPhoto.com/CEmoryMoody, 18; BigStockPhoto.com/Global Photographers, 12–13;
Brand X Pictures, 24; Dreamstime/Omar Ariff Kamarul Ariffin, 15; Dreamstime/Pufferfishy,
22; iStockphoto/John Pitcher, cover (badger); iStockphoto/Markanja, 9; iStockphoto/Pavlo
Maydikov, cover (ostrich); iStockphoto/Ryan KC Wong, 12; Peter Arnold/A. Visage, 6; Peter
Arnold/D. Tipling, 10; Peter Arnold/S. Muller, 24–25; Peter Arnold/Steven Kazlowski, 7;
SeaPics.com/Doug Perrine, 22–23; Shutterstock/Alexander Kolomietz, 1 (middle), 2
(bottom); Shutterstock/Alexey Biryukov, 2 (top); Shutterstock/Alexey Kryuchkov, 27
(bottom); Shutterstock/Dan Bannister, 4; Shutterstock/Daniel Gale, 18–19; Shutterstock/
Eline Spek, 27 (top); Shutterstock/EML, 3 (middle right); Shutterstock/Eric Lawton, 17;
Shutterstock/Eugene Buchko, 20; Shutterstock/Jan Martin Will, 1 (right), 3 (bottom);
Shutterstock/Joe Gough, 8; Shutterstock/John Bell, 16; Shutterstock/Juha Tuomi, 26
(bottom); Shutterstock/Loke Yek Mang, 3 (top); Shutterstock/Robynrg, 29; Shutterstock/
Ryan Arnaudin, 14–15; Shutterstock/Sara Robinson, 27 (middle right); Shutterstock/
Shironina Lidiya Alexandrovna, 1 (left), 26 (top); Shutterstock/Stanislav Khrapov, 4–5;
Shutterstock/Steffen Foerster Photography, 11; Shutterstock/Wesley Aston, 20–21

Note to Parents, Teachers, and Librarians
This Animal Opposites book uses full-color photographs and a nonfiction format
to introduce children to the concepts of short and tall. *Short and Tall* is designed to
be read aloud to a pre-reader or to be read independently by an early reader.
Photographs help listeners and early readers understand the text and concepts
discussed. The book encourages further learning by including the following
sections: Did You Know?, Glossary, Read More, Internet Sites, and Index. Early
readers may need assistance using these features.